The Urbana Free Library

To renew: call **217-367-4057**
or go to **urbanafreelibrary.org**
and select **My Account**

Earth Day

by Meg Gaertner

FOCUS READERS

SCOUT

www.focusreaders.com

Focus Readers is distributed by North Star Editions:
sales@northstareditions.com | 888-417-0195

Produced for Focus Readers by Red Line Editorial.

Photographs ©: Wavebreakmedia/iStockphoto, cover, 1; JPL/NASA, 4, 16 (top left); Steve Debenport/iStockphoto, 7; vovashevchuk/iStockphoto, 9 (top), 16 (top right); Phonix_a/iStockphoto, 9 (bottom); yulkapopkova/iStockphoto, 11; Zinkevych/iStockphoto, 13 (top); FatCamera/iStockphoto, 13 (bottom); monkeybusinessimages/iStockphoto, 15; yoh4nn/iStockphoto, 16 (bottom left); Knaupe/iStockphoto, 16 (bottom right).

Library of Congress Cataloging-in-Publication Data
Library of Congress Cataloging-in-Publication Data is available on the Library of Congress website.

ISBN
978-1-64493-020-5 (hardcover)
978-1-64493-099-1 (paperback)
978-1-64493-257-5 (ebook pdf)
978-1-64493-178-3 (hosted ebook)

Printed in the United States of America
Mankato, MN
012020

About the Author

Meg Gaertner is a children's book editor and author. She lives in Minneapolis, Minnesota. When not writing, she is usually dancing or spending time outside.

Table of Contents

Earth

Our Home

Earth Day is in April.

Earth is our home.

We help Earth.

We work together.

We keep Earth clean.

We keep Earth beautiful.

Helping Earth

Some people drop **trash**.

The land gets dirty.

The water gets dirty.

trash

We get trash bags.

We pick up trash.

We clean the land.

trash bag

We plant a **tree**.

We plant a **garden**.

tree

garden

Beautiful Earth

We go outside.

We enjoy Earth.

Earth is beautiful.

Glossary

Earth

trash

garden

tree

Index

16